RAINY DAYS

PUPPETS

DENNY ROBSON
AND
VANESSA BAILEY

GLOUCESTER PRESS
New York · London · Toronto · Sydney

CONTENTS

Design: David West
             Children's Book Design
Photography: Roger Vlitos

© Aladdin Books Ltd 1990

*First published in
the United States in 1991 by*
Gloucester Press
387 Park Avenue South
New York, NY 10016

Library of Congress Cataloging-in-
Publication Data

Bailey, Vanessa.
    Puppets : games and projects / Vanessa
    Bailey.
       p.cm. -- (Rainy days)
    Includes index.
    Summary: Explains how to make and
    operate several types of puppets and
    includes instructions on preparing and
    presenting a puppet theater show.
       ISBN 0-531-17269-4
       1. Puppet theater--Juvenile literature.
    2. Puppet making--Juvenile literature.
    [1. Puppets. 2. Puppet making. 3. Puppet
    theater.] I. Title. II. Series: Bailey, Vanessa.
    Rainy days.
    PN1972.B225   1991
    791.5'3--dc20   90-44841   CIP   AC

Introduction

All through the ages, from the ancient Chinese to the Romans, people have used puppets to entertain themselves and to tell stories.

This book shows you how to make many different kinds of puppets and how to work them. They range from the very simply made glove and sock puppets, like Angry Andy and Hissing Sid, to the more complicated designs of the stick puppets, like our Bee-bothered Orchestra Conductor, and the marionettes.

Most of the puppets in this book are theater puppets — they can be brought to life and used in puppet shows. Read on and find out how to make a puppet theater and how to put on a play. With a little imagination, a few household odds and ends, and perhaps a helper or two, you can become a puppeteer as well as puppet-maker.

Here are some of the materials that we used to create the puppets in this book. You will probably be able to find many of the things you need at home, like old socks or gloves, scraps of yarn or garden stakes. The other items are not expensive to buy.

You could start making a collection of odds and ends that you think may be useful for puppet-making. Then you will be ready to create your own puppet designs when you have a little experience.

Dancing Dandy

Dancing Dandy is a puppet toy, rather than a puppet that acts in a puppet theater. You can have fun making him for yourself or you could make him to give as a present. Once you have mastered the Dancing Dandy, you can use the same idea to make other dancing puppet toys, such as a ballerina or a clown. Use the Dancing Dandy pattern on page 32 to draw the basic outline or make up your own.

You will need cardboard, string, brass paper fasteners, scotch tape or strong glue, paints or felt-tip pens to decorate.

HOW TO WORK THE DANDY
Hold the string at the top and bottom of the puppet. Gently pull and release the string so that the arms and legs dance in and out.

1 Trace the pattern shapes onto thin cardboard and carefully cut them out. Decorate and make holes for the string and fasteners as shown.

1

2 Put the Dandy together with paper fasteners, making sure that his arms and legs can move freely.

2

3 Use fine string to join the arms together and the legs together.

3

4

4 Attach a string to the head. With the arms and legs in the outstretched position, tie another piece of string to link the arms and legs.

Swinging monkey

Like the Dancing Dandy, the swinging monkey is a puppet toy. He's quite easy to make, yet his acrobatics are very impressive. You can use the pattern on page 32 to trace the basic shape. If you design your own monkey, make sure his arms are longer than his body.

You will need cardboard, two sticks, string, a paper fastener, glue, two sections cut from a drinking straw, paints or felt-tip pens.

HOW THE MONKEY WORKS

Hold a stick in each hand. Move the tops of the sticks away from each other and the monkey will swing up. As he reaches the top, move the sticks together slightly and he will swing over. Repeat this and the monkey will swing over backward.

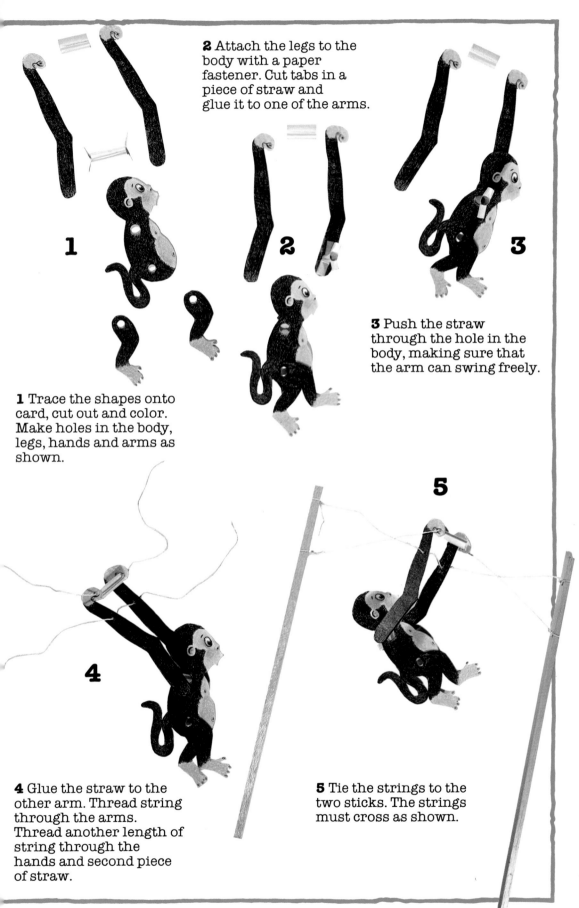

2 Attach the legs to the body with a paper fastener. Cut tabs in a piece of straw and glue it to one of the arms.

1

2

3

1 Trace the shapes onto card, cut out and color. Make holes in the body, legs, hands and arms as shown.

3 Push the straw through the hole in the body, making sure that the arm can swing freely.

5

4

4 Glue the straw to the other arm. Thread string through the arms. Thread another length of string through the hands and second piece of straw.

5 Tie the strings to the two sticks. The strings must cross as shown.

Cardboard theater

You can have a lot of fun both making and using this cardboard theater. If you make different kinds of scenery backdrops and a number of puppets, you can perform lots of different plays. You could act out traditional fairy tales, (we have used the story of Goldilocks and the Three Bears in our theater), Greek myths, fables, a combination of lots of tales, or your own made-up stories.

You will need a few sheets of thin white cardboard, strong glue or scotch tape and bright paints or felt-tip pens to decorate.

HOW THE THEATER WORKS

Work out your story in advance and decide in which order the characters should appear. It's a good idea to get a friend to help with the performance. Then you can use two puppets each, which means there can be lots of action on the stage at the same time.

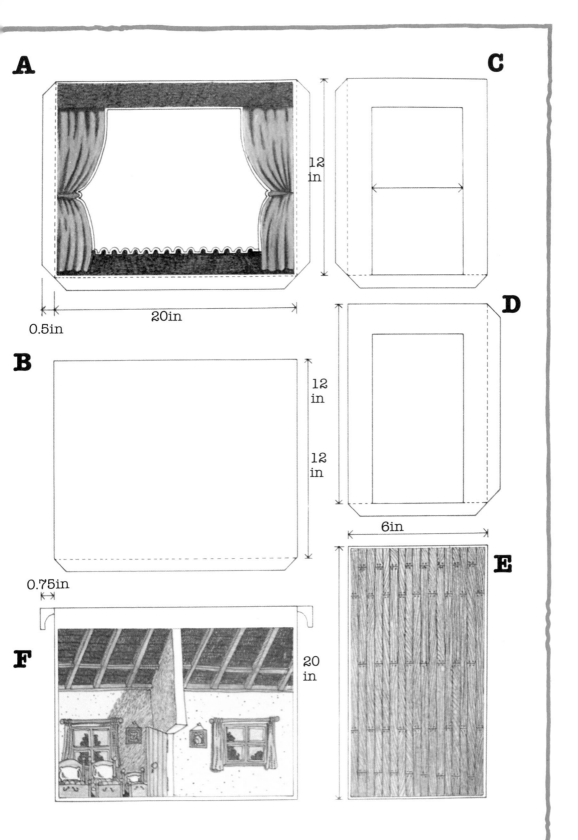

A

12 in

20in

0.5in

B

0.75in

C

D

12 in

12 in

6in

E

F

20 in

Cut out the front (**A**), the back (**B**), the sides (**C, D**), the floor (**E**) and the scenery (**F**). Cut out the stage and side openings and decorate.

If you can't get hold of white cardboard to make the theater, you could use a cardboard box for the basic structure and drop in the scenery as shown.

Cardboard theater

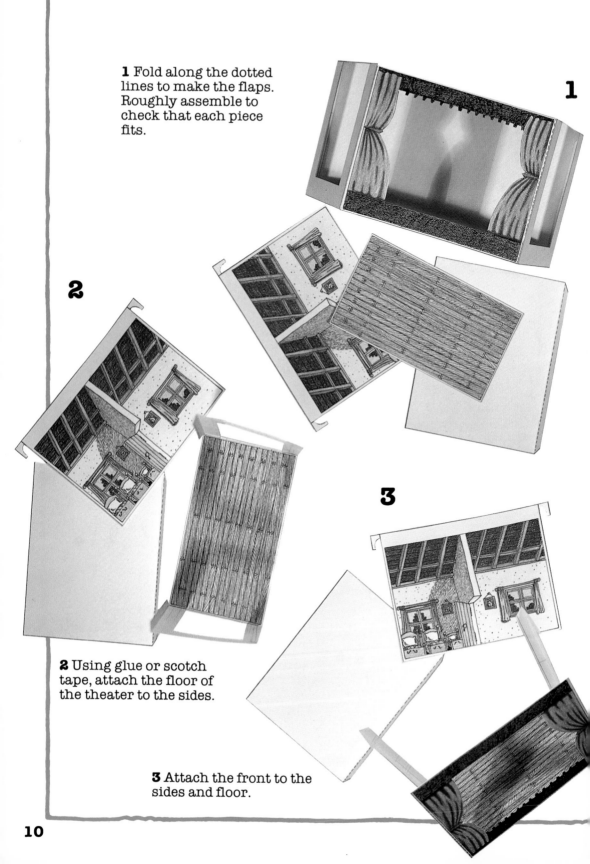

1 Fold along the dotted lines to make the flaps. Roughly assemble to check that each piece fits.

2 Using glue or scotch tape, attach the floor of the theater to the sides.

3 Attach the front to the sides and floor.

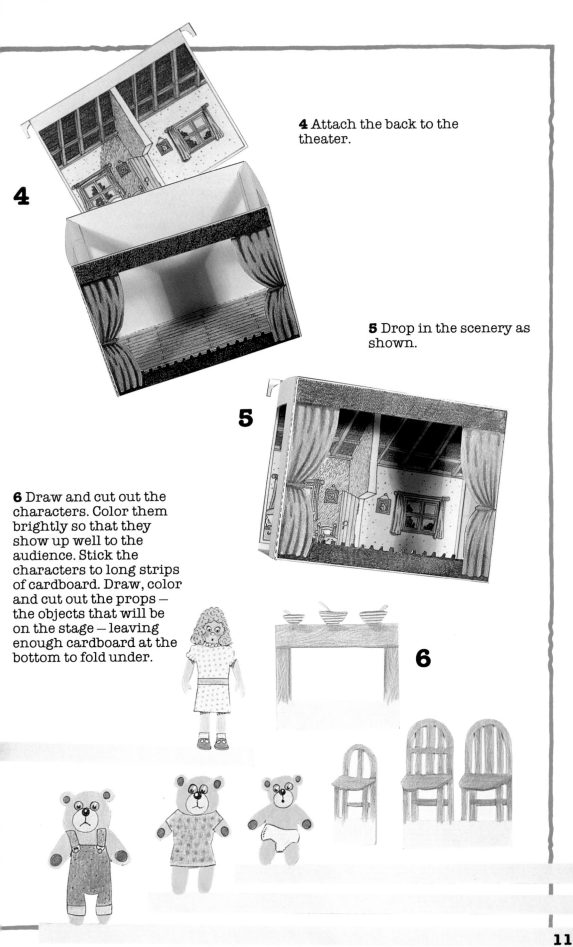

4 Attach the back to the theater.

4

5 Drop in the scenery as shown.

5

6 Draw and cut out the characters. Color them brightly so that they show up well to the audience. Stick the characters to long strips of cardboard. Draw, color and cut out the props — the objects that will be on the stage — leaving enough cardboard at the bottom to fold under.

6

Sock puppets

Sock puppets are some of the more simple puppets to make and yet they can be brought to life very easily and effectively. They can move about, have a whole range of different expressions and of course you can make them speak!

You will need some old socks, yarn, string, plasticine, glue, gummed labels, ping-pong balls or cotton balls, felt, cardboard and pens to decorate.

HISSING SID

HOW SOCK PUPPETS WORK

Put your hand in the sock puppet with your thumb underneath the mouth and the rest of your fingers above. Make the puppet nod by bending your wrist. Open and close his mouth by moving your fingers and thumb as you talk. You can give him some funny expressions by scrunching up your hand.

KEEP-FIT POODLE
This strange hound has a yellow felt sweatband to keep his black yarn hair out of his eyes.

HUMPHREY HEDGEHOG
This prickly creature has yellow yarn spikes, a red felt tongue and gummed label eyes.

DIGBY DOGFISH
Digby swims on stage with a blue sock body, black felt hair and blue felt fins.

How to make Hissing Sid

You need a green sock for Hissing Sid's snaky body, green yarn for his hair, some string, cotton balls or ping-pong balls and modeling clay for his eyes, red felt for his tongue, cardboard, felt-tip pens and strong glue.

1 Cut several lengths of yarn and tie at one end with string. Cut a hole in the top of the sock.

1

2

2 Push the tied end of the yarn into the hole and tie a piece of string around the sock to secure it. Make the mouth from cardboard and add a felt tongue.

3 Glue the mouth onto the sock.

3

4

4 Make the eyes from the balls and plasticine and glue them onto the sock.

Glove puppets

Like sock puppets, glove puppets are very easy to make and they are also excellent performers in a puppet show. They don't have moveable mouths like the sock puppets, but they can pick up props and suggest a wide range of moods by using their hands and arms. You don't have to cut up old gloves to make these puppets as you use an old sock for the head and body.

You will need gloves, old socks, yarn, cotton balls, colored felt, string, paper, glue, gummed labels and felt-tip pens.

HOW GLOVE PUPPETS WORK
Put your gloved hand in the sock so that your forefinger is in the head and your middle finger and thumb become the arms. The puppet can twist its body, bow, nod its head, clap hands and pick up props.

PATRICIA PANDA

KEVIN THE CLOWN
This jolly circus character is brightly colored, with his blue body, green hair and yellow hat. His big red nose is a cotton ball.

ANGRY ANDY
This fearsome fellow looks mean and moody. His wild black yarn hair is stuck out with hairspray.

FIONA FAIRFLAX
The fair Fiona has been given a startled expression with gummed label eyes and mouth.

How to make Fiona Fairflax

You need a pink sock and glove for Fiona's body and arms, yellow yarn for her hair, string, paper, yarn, gummed labels and felt-tip pens.

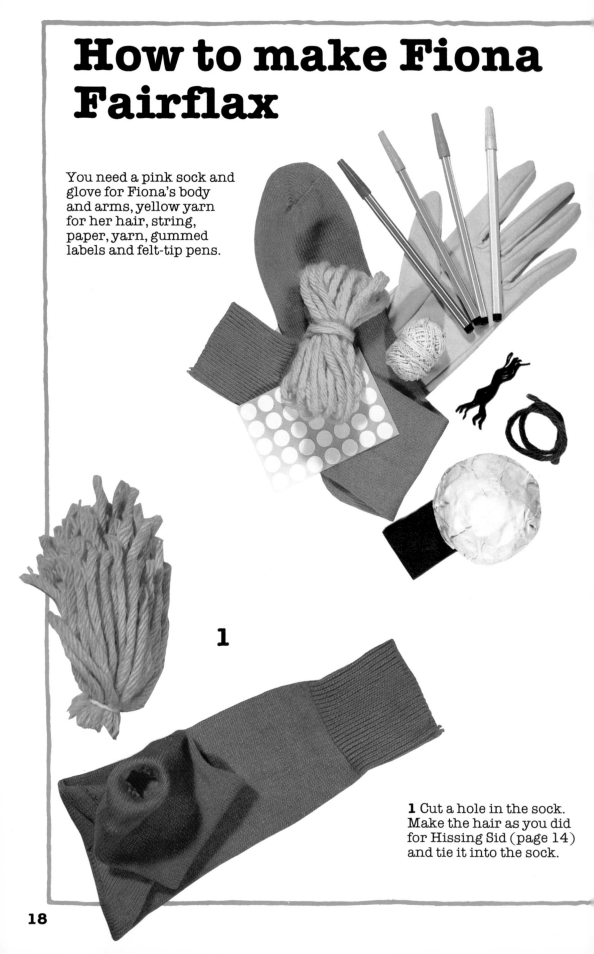

1

1 Cut a hole in the sock. Make the hair as you did for Hissing Sid (page 14) and tie it into the sock.

2 Scrunch up a ball of paper, leaving a hole in which to put your finger. Put the ball in the sock and tie loosely with yarn.

2

3

3 Make Fiona's face from gummed labels and use black yarn to make her eyelashes.

4 Cut holes in either side of the sock where you think her arms should go. You can cover the holes with strips of felt.

4

5

5 Trim hair to style, put on the glove and Fiona is ready!

Stick puppets

This strange band of musicians with their conductor are all stick puppets. You can make this kind of puppet as complicated or as simple as you like. Our puppets each have two sticks, with one stick operating an arm and one supporting the body. You can make stick puppets with many moving parts – although you may need an assistant or two to help you operate them.

You will need dowels, balsa wood or garden stakes, (long pencils can also be used), colored felt, drawing pins, yarn, cotton balls or ping-pong balls, plasticine, cardboard and pens.

HOW STICK PUPPETS WORK
These puppets are very simple to operate. You hold the stick that supports the body with one hand, while moving the other stick around so that the puppet moves its arm.

THE BEE-BOTHERED CONDUCTOR
Our conductor is trying to swat a bee with his baton, much to the confusion of the musicians!

CHARLOTTE THE CELLIST
Charlotte plays her cello by moving the bow in her left hand.

GUY THE GUITARIST
Guy plays the guitar by strumming it with his right hand.

DENISE THE DRUMMER
Denise beats on the drums as her felt arms flap up and down.

How to make the conductor

To make the conductor you will need a long, sharpened pencil or balsa wood stick for the support, a thinner stick, a cotton ball or ping-pong ball for the head, yarn for the hair, a plasticine nose, felt, a drawing pin, white cardboard and a felt-tip pen.

1

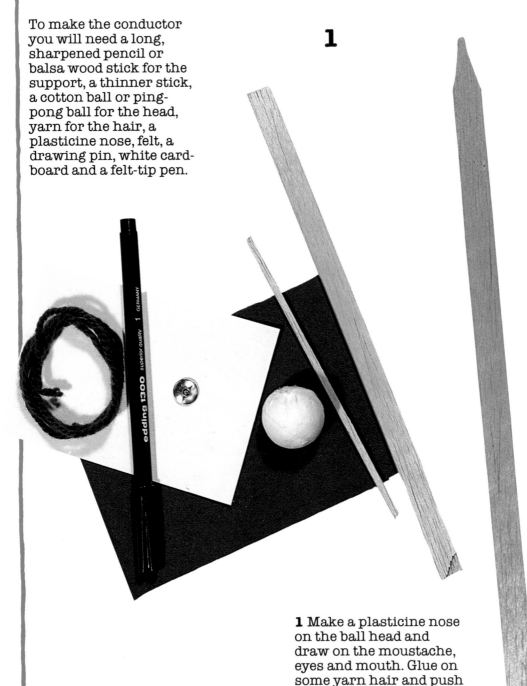

1 Make a plasticine nose on the ball head and draw on the moustache, eyes and mouth. Glue on some yarn hair and push a pointed stick into the head.

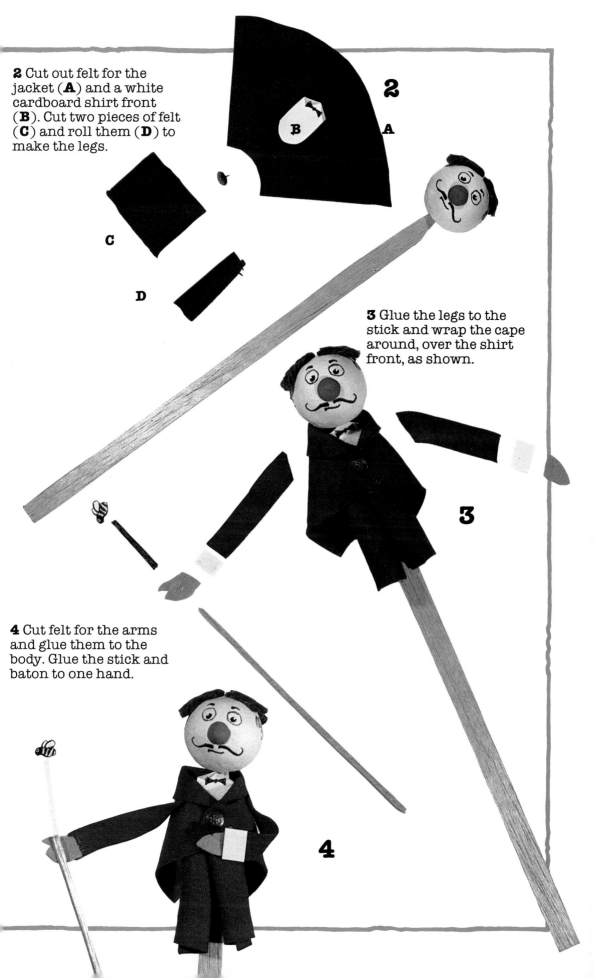

2 Cut out felt for the jacket (**A**) and a white cardboard shirt front (**B**). Cut two pieces of felt (**C**) and roll them (**D**) to make the legs.

2

B A

C

D

3 Glue the legs to the stick and wrap the cape around, over the shirt front, as shown.

3

4 Cut felt for the arms and glue them to the body. Glue the stick and baton to one hand.

4

Marionettes

Marionettes are string puppets that are worked from above. Like many other kinds of puppets, marionettes have been used to entertain people all over the world for hundreds of years. Here are some simple examples for you to make to add to your puppet show.

You will need dowels or balsa wood sticks, string, ping-pong balls or cotton balls, colored felt, strong glue, plasticine, cardboard and felt-tip pens to decorate.

THE FUNKY CHICKEN

HOW MARIONETTES WORK

To operate a marionette you tilt the crosspiece in various directions so that the puppet walks, dances, pecks or flies. The more strings the puppet has, the more complicated it is to control, so practice in front of a mirror before you give your performance.

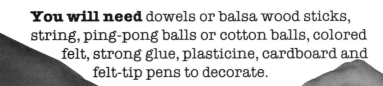

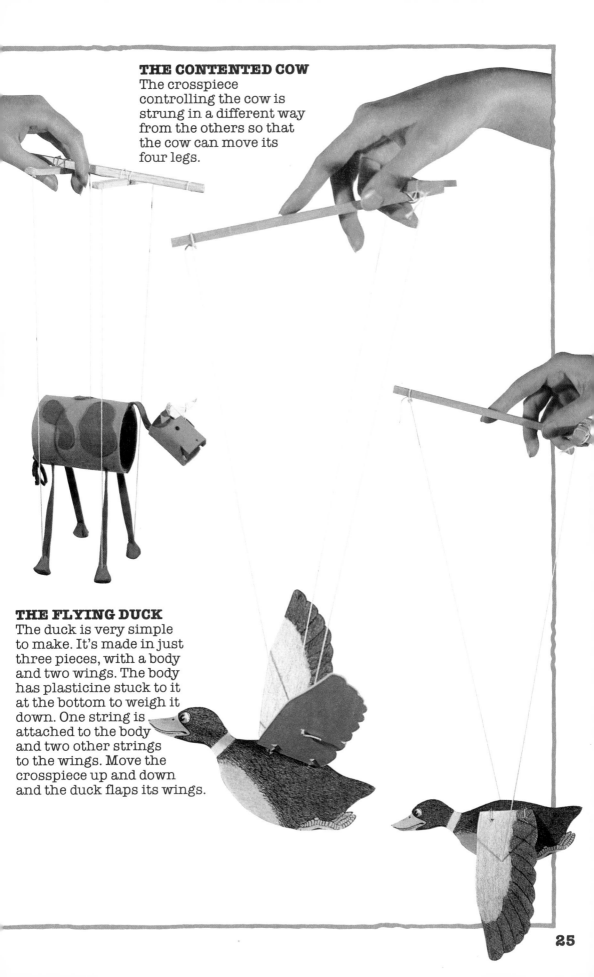

THE CONTENTED COW

The crosspiece controlling the cow is strung in a different way from the others so that the cow can move its four legs.

THE FLYING DUCK

The duck is very simple to make. It's made in just three pieces, with a body and two wings. The body has plasticine stuck to it at the bottom to weigh it down. One string is attached to the body and two other strings to the wings. Move the crosspiece up and down and the duck flaps its wings.

How to make the chicken

1

The funky chicken is made from colored felt, yarn, two sticks, two ping-pong balls or cotton balls, plasticine, string, a paper fastener, glue, cardboard and pens to decorate.

1 Use plasticine for the feet, beak and eyes, yarn for the neck and legs, felt for the comb and put together as shown.

2

2 Wrap a piece of yellow felt around the other cotton ball for the body. Glue on felt wings and a cardboard collar and tie.

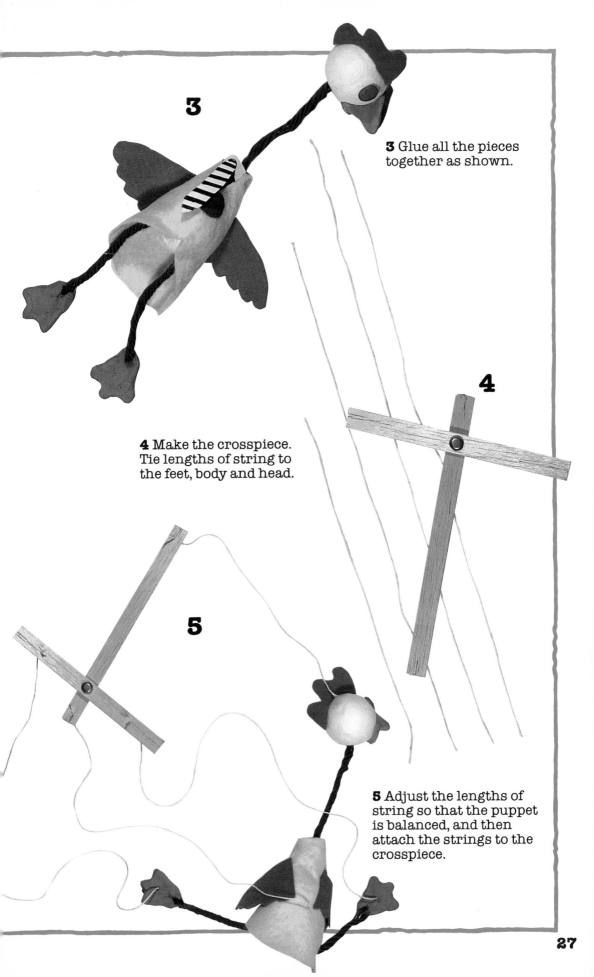

3 Glue all the pieces together as shown.

4 Make the crosspiece. Tie lengths of string to the feet, body and head.

5 Adjust the lengths of string so that the puppet is balanced, and then attach the strings to the crosspiece.

Making a puppet theater

Once you have made your puppets, it's time to bring them to life. Of course, you don't have to have a special theater for your puppets to perform in. You could simply crouch down behind a sofa and hold up your glove, sock or stick puppets. Or you could make a very simple theater by using a couple of kitchen chairs covered with an old tablecloth to hide the puppeteers from the audience.

But if you want a more permanent theater, here is a design that is easy to make. As this theater folds up, it doesn't take up much space and you can take it anywhere you go.

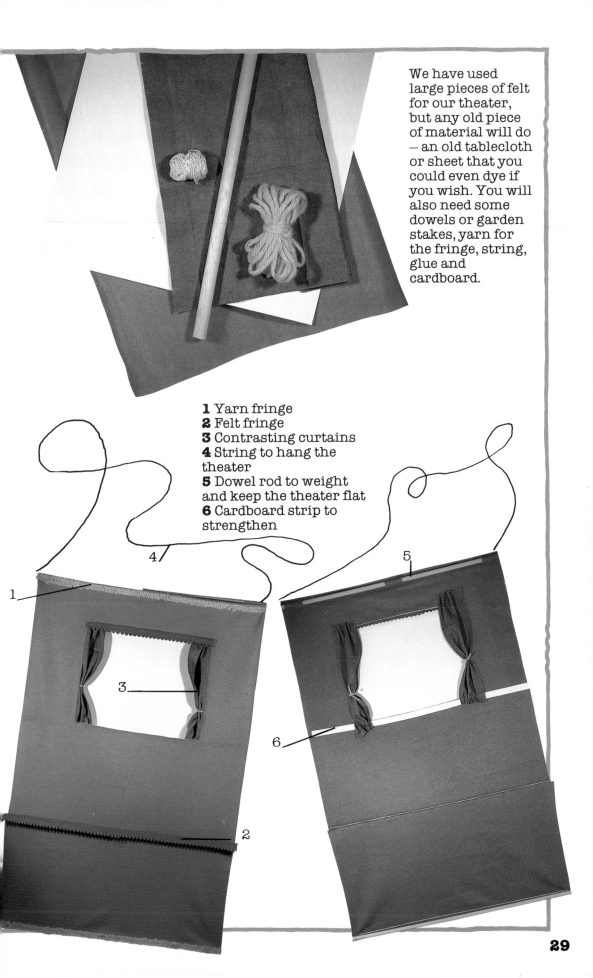

We have used large pieces of felt for our theater, but any old piece of material will do — an old tablecloth or sheet that you could even dye if you wish. You will also need some dowels or garden stakes, yarn for the fringe, string, glue and cardboard.

1 Yarn fringe
2 Felt fringe
3 Contrasting curtains
4 String to hang the theater
5 Dowel rod to weight and keep the theater flat
6 Cardboard strip to strengthen

The play

Now you are ready to put your play together. First decide on your storyline, which of the puppets you want in the play and how many helpers you need. It's a good idea to write out a script, listing the scenes and what happens in each, so that you know in what order the puppets appear and who does what.

Remember, puppets like to do things, so think about what kind of characters they are and keep them moving!

Here is a script of a "Punch and Judy" type play involving some of the puppets in the book. When you create your plays write out a script like this and tape it to the back of the theater. Make sure you have all the puppets and any props ready before you begin.

SCRIPT

Scene 1 (**Use tape recorder**) Musicians play and then begin making awful noise (**do sound effects**) as conductor waves his baton at the bee.

Scene 2 Hedgehog arrives and says there is a mystery guest coming, but he doesn't know where he is. Asks audience to shout if they see anyone. Kevin Clown appears behind him, doing silly things.

Scene 3 Hedgehog turns around but the clown has gone. Repeat this several times.

Scene 4 Panda tries to tell him the clown has arrived, but as she can't speak the hedgehog doesn't understand.

Scene 5 Panda gets annoyed because hedgehog always looks the wrong way.

Scene 6 Hedgehog finally turns and sees the clown!

he musicians screech to a halt
ithout their conductor.

"Tonight we have a mystery guest...
but I seem to have lost him."

said only shout out if you see the
ystery guest!"

"What are you trying to tell me? Who
has arrived? I can't see anyone."

anda gets more and more angry as
edgehog fails to see the clown.

"So there you are. Now why didn't
anyone tell me you were here?"

Pattern help

Trace these shapes onto cardboard to make the Dancing Dandy and the Swinging Monkey.

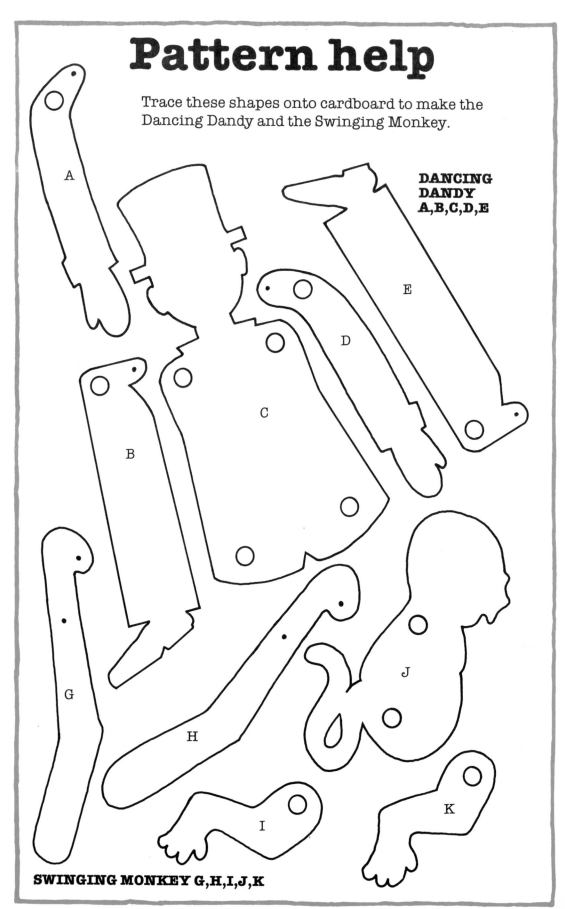

DANCING DANDY A,B,C,D,E

SWINGING MONKEY G,H,I,J,K

PRINTED IN BELGIUM BY proost INTERNATIONAL BOOK PRODUCTION